I Want to Be an Astronaut   by Byron Barton

Thomas Y. Crowell   New York
A Harcourt Brace & Company Edition

I Want to Be an Astronaut Copyright © 1988 by Byron Barton Printed in the U.S.A. All rights reserved.   4 5 6 7 8 9 10
Library of Congress Cataloging-in-Publication Data Barton, Byron. I want to be an astronaut. Summary: A young child wants to be an astronaut and
goes on a mission into space. [1. Astronautics—Fiction] I. Title. PZ7.B2848Iwa 1988 [E] 87-24311   ISBN 0-15-302115-2

I want to be an astronaut,

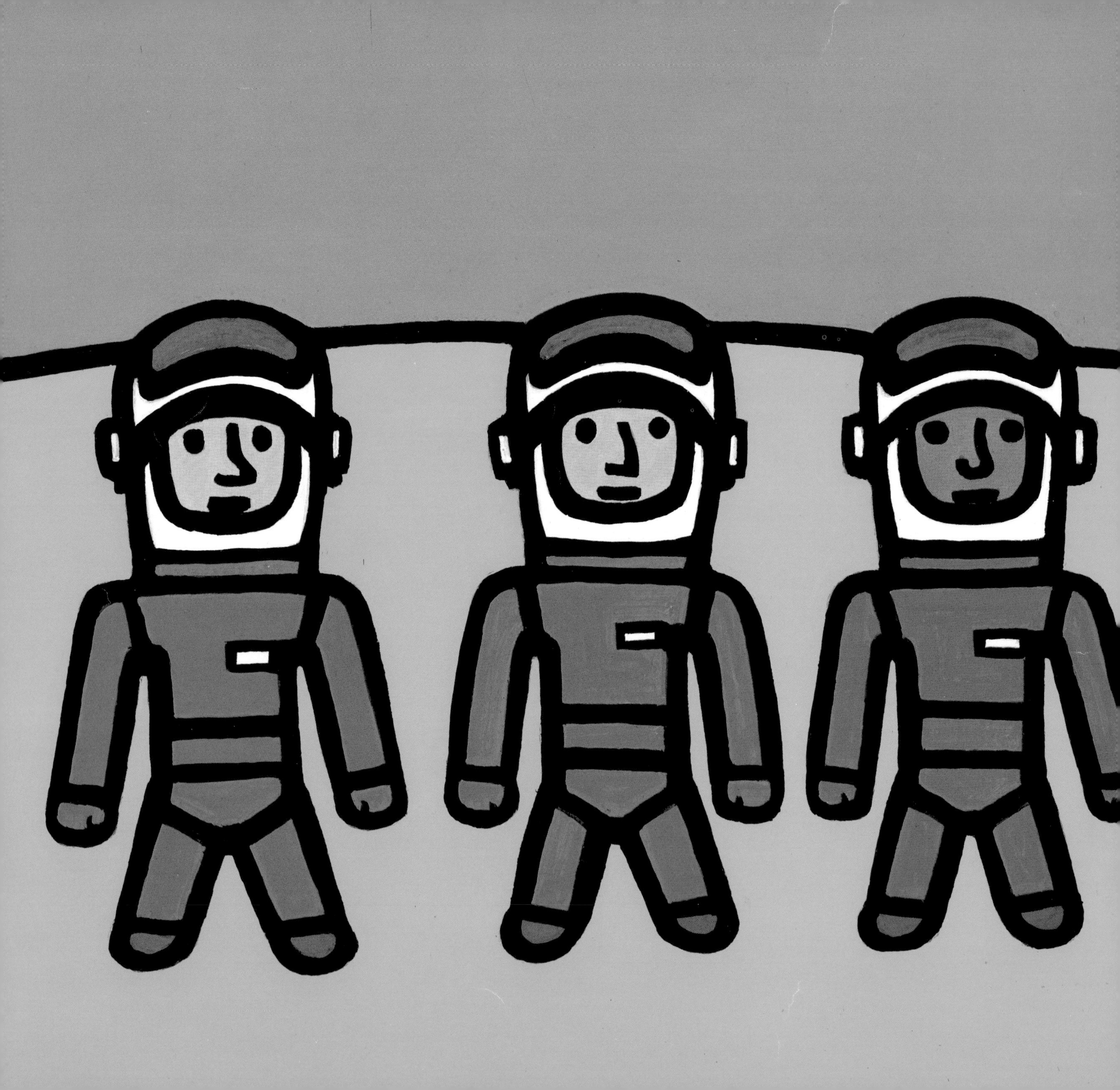

a member of the crew,

and fly on the shuttle

I want to be up there

on a space mission

and have ready-to-eat meals

and sleep in zero gravity.

I want to put on a space suit

and walk around in space

and help fix a satellite

and build a factory in orbit.

I want to be up there awhile

and then come back to Earth.

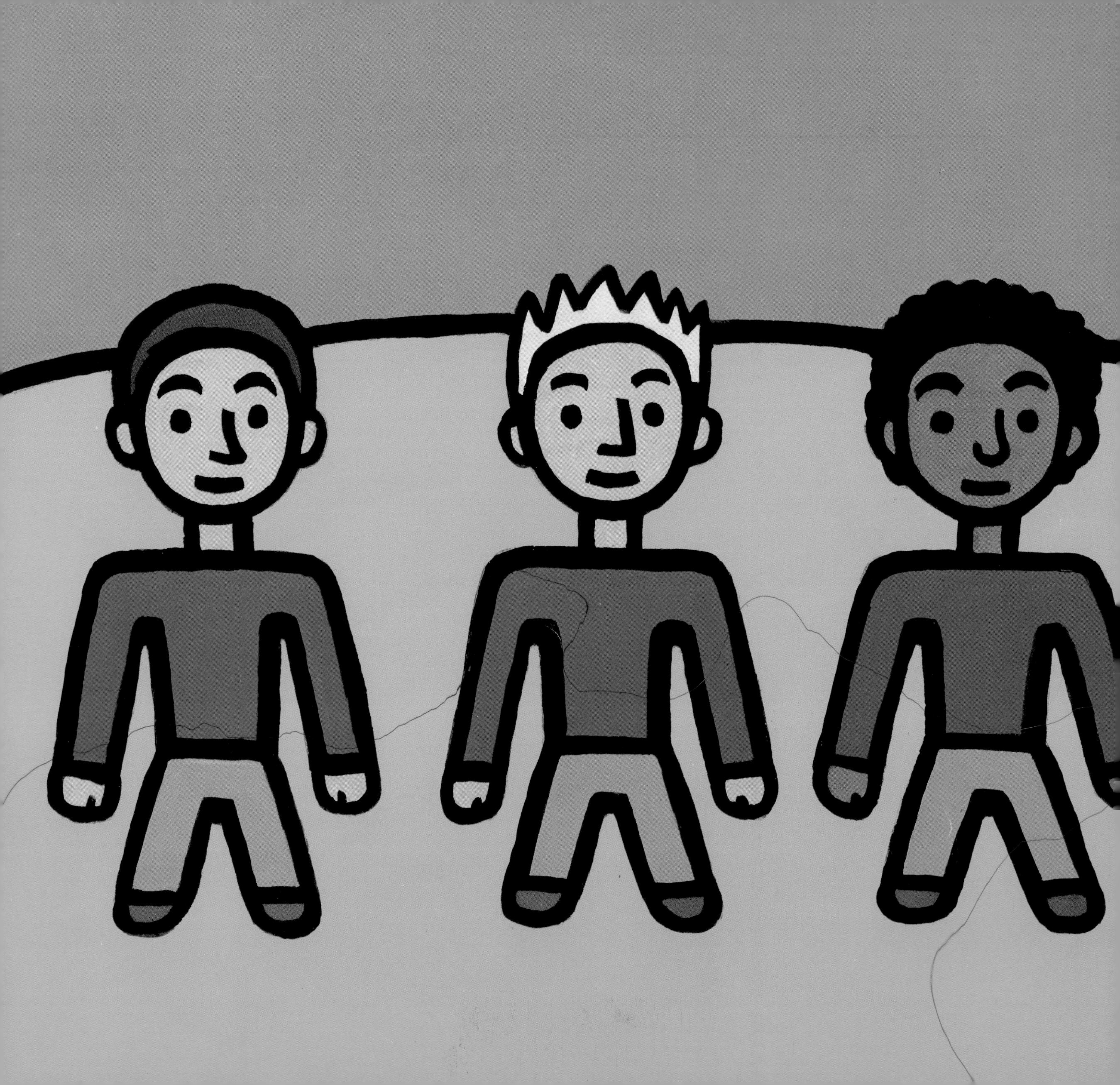

I just want to be an astronaut

and visit outer space.